OMAHA BEACH
NORMANDY 1944

Leo Marriott and Simon Forty

Casemate
PHILADELPHIA & OXFORD

Published in the United States of America and Great Britain in 2016
by CASEMATE PUBLISHERS
1950 Lawrence Road, Havertown, PA 19083
and 10 Hythe Bridge Street, Oxford, OX1 2EW

ISBN-13: 978-1-61200-425-9

Produced by Greene Media Ltd.

Cataloging-in-publication data is available from the Library of Congress
and the British Library.

10 9 8 7 6 5 4 3 2 1

Printed and bound in China
For a complete list of Casemate titles please contact:
CASEMATE PUBLISHERS (US)
Telephone (610) 853-9131, Fax (610) 853-9146
E-mail: casemate@casematepublishers.com

CASEMATE PUBLISHERS (UK)
Telephone (01865) 241249, Fax (01865) 794449
E-mail: casemate-uk@casematepublishers.co.uk

Acknowledgments
Most of the photos are US Signal Corps images that have come from a
number of sources. Grateful thanks go to BattlefieldHistorian.com, NARA
College Park, MD, and the George Forty Library for historic photos; other
credits are noted on the photographs—WikiCommons has proved
extremely useful. If anyone is missing or incorrectly credited, apologies:
please notify the authors through the publishers.

I'd like to thank in particular Leo Marriott for the aerial photography. Other
thanks are due to Michel Le Querrec, Mark Franklin (maps), Ian Hughes
(design) Richard Wood and the military cyclists (particularly Peter Anderson)
for photos and enthusiasm.

Previous page:
The armada sails. Portsmouth's D-Day Museum reports that Operation
Neptune included nearly 7,000 vessels: 1,213 naval combat ships, 4,126
landing ships and landing craft, 736 ancillary craft and 864 merchant vessels.

Right:
View over Omaha Beach from WN60, F–1 draw in the foreground.

Contents

Introduction

Above:
"The Big Red One" and the 116th RCT from the 29th Infantry Division comprised the first wave of troops that assaulted on Omaha Beach. In spite of heavy casualties, the division took Formigny by the end of the first day.

Below:
The huge losses suffered by 29th Infantry Division's A Company, 1/116th Infantry, from the Virginia National Guard in Bedford, VA, led to it being selected for the site of the National D-Day Memorial.

OF THE FIVE Normandy beaches attacked on June 6, Omaha saw the highest Allied casualties. As has been so graphically portrayed in *Saving Private Ryan*, the initial attack foundered. Well-placed defenders with the high ground, inaccurate Allied bombardments, extensive beach defenses, murderous and concentrated fire—all did their job. On top of this, Allied intelligence had missed the arrival of 352. Infanterie-division, which reached full strength in March, complete with its divisional artillery of Eastern Front veterans. As Steven Zaloga put it in *The Devil's Garden*, his excellent analysis of the German side of the battle, "Instead of facing only three companies of infantry, the U.S. Army unexpectedly faced a defending force about three times its size and much better armed."

So much went wrong with the first wave. Many of the amphibious Sherman DD tanks of the 741st Tank Bn didn't reach the beach. They were released from their landing craft too far from shore where the greater swell swamped them, and the troops landing on Omaha missed their firepower. The same was true of the first wave's artillery: only one of the 105mm howitzers of the 11th FA Bn reached shore by DUKW; six of the 7th Bn's guns suffered the same fate.

Another problem was that many units landed in the wrong place. Strong tides and winds swept the landing craft off line and led to confusion. The engineers and naval demolition parties who were supposed to blow gaps in the beach obstacles took fearful casualties (41% of the Army-Navy Special Engineer Task Force). Only six of sixteen dozers reached the shore and three were almost immediately disabled by artillery. Fifteen officers and men of the demolition parties of all ranks were awarded the Distinguished Service Cross for their bravery.

Finally, the German emplacements and defenses had been well sited on high ground and the only cover on the beach—the seawall—was over a killing ground. Rommel realized how tempting this beach would be for the Allies and had ensured it was more than well protected. There were 32 fortified areas located between the Vire River and Port-en-Bessin: in all, 12 of these strongpoints were able to direct fire on Omaha Beach. The beaches were also covered by inland artillery and mortars, all zoned in to the killing ground.

The attacking forces—the 29th Infantry Division and the veteran 1st Infantry, the "Big Red One"—suffered over 2,000 casualties. However, as annihilation seemed inevitable, and General Omar Bradley, watching from USS *Augusta*, "contemplated the diversion of Omaha follow-up forces to Utah or the British beaches," the men on shore, led by US Rangers, themselves misplaced (they were the follow-up troops to Rudder's Rangers who had scaled the Pointe du Hoc), pushed forward. Bravery under fire and an indomitable will to win saw small units infiltrate the bluffs and strike inland.

They were helped in no small part by the destroyers offshore, which approached suicidally close to the beach to provide covering fire, and by the few tanks that had been landed and survived the attentions of the German antitank and artillery. The Germans faltered under the bombardment. As they ran short of ammunition, their morale was further knocked as information about the successful landings on Sword Beach to the east were reported by Infantry Regiment 726 at around 08:00. By 09:00 the *Widerstandsnester*—resistance points—had begun to fall. And the American troops kept landing. By nightfall, they had gained hold of the beach and its immediate hinterland. Despite the resistance and the casualties, 34,000 troops had arrived over Omaha Beach.

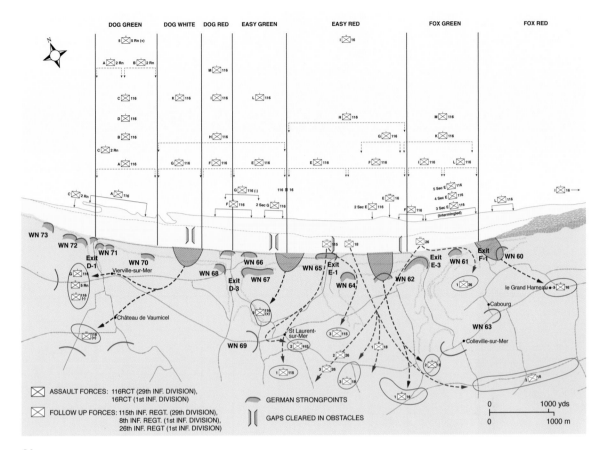

DOG GREEN   DOG WHITE   DOG RED   EASY GREEN   EASY RED   FOX GREEN   FOX RED

WN 73
WN 72
WN 71
Exit D-1
WN 70
Vierville-sur-Mer
Château de Vaumicel
WN 68
WN 66
WN 67
Exit D-3
WN 69
St Laurent-sur-Mer
WN 65
Exit E-1
WN 64
WN 62
WN 63
Colleville-sur-Mer
Exit E-3
WN 61
WN 60
Exit F-1
le Grand Hameau
Cabourg

⊠ ASSAULT FORCES: 116RCT (29th INF. DIVISION),
    16RCT (1st INF. DIVISION)

⊠ FOLLOW UP FORCES: 115th INF. REGT. (29th DIVISION),
    8th INF. REGT. (1st INF. DIVISION),
    26th INF. REGT. (1st INF. DIVISION)

GERMAN STRONGPOINTS

GAPS CLEARED IN OBSTACLES

0   1000 yds
0   1000 m

Above:

The plan for the landings proved to be optimistic as foretold by 29th Division's Asst Div CO, Norman Cota:"This is different from any of the other exercises that you've had so far....You're going to find confusion. The landing craft aren't going in on schedule and people are going to be landed in the wrong place. Some won't be landed at all....We must improvise, carry on, not lose our heads." The primary objective at Omaha was to secure a beachhead of some 5 miles (8km) depth, between Port-en-Bessin and the Vire River, linking with the British landings at Gold to the east, and reaching the area of Isigny to the west to link up with VII Corps landing at Utah, although the stern defense meant this didn't take place for a few days. That it happened at all was in no small part thanks to "Dutch" Cota who led the way off the beach earning the DSC in the process.

Right:
This photo shows well the dominant bluffs and mass of stakes and defenses on the shoreline.

Left:
Aerial view of Vierville-sur-Mer looking towards Les Moulins showing the extent of the beach at low water.

Below:
The sweeping curve of Omaha Beach stretching from D–1 draw at Vierville (at **A**), past Les Moulins (D–3, at **C**), Le Ruquet (E–1, at **D**), to E–3 (**E**) and F–1 (**F**). At **B** the two cliff-mounted MG positions shown on p 31.

OMAHA LANDINGS ORDER OF BATTLE

First US Army: Lt-Gen. Omar N. Bradley   V Corps: Maj-Gen. Leonard T. Gerow

1st Inf Div: Maj-Gen. Clarence R. Huebner	Special Engineer Task Force: Col. John T. O'Neil
29th Inf Div: Maj-Gen. Charles H. Gerhardt	3rd Armored Group: Col. Severan D. McLaughlin
2nd Inf Div: Maj-Gen. Walter M. Robertson	Provisional Engineer Special Brigade Group: Brig-Gen.
Provisional Ranger Group: Lt-Col. James E. Rudder	William M. Hoge

16th RCT of 1st Inf Div	116th RCT of 29th Inf Div	Follow up units
16th Inf Regt	116th Inf Regt	**18th RCT of 1st Inf Div**
741st Tk Bn	C Coy, 2nd Ranger Bn	18th Inf Regt
Special Engr Task Force	5th Ranger Bn	745th Tk Bn
7th Fd Arty Bn	743rd Tk Bn	32nd and 5th Fd Arty Bn
62nd Armd Fd Arty Bn	Special Engr Task Force	5th ESB
197th AAA Bn	111th Fd Arty Bn	
1st Engr Bn	58th Armd Fd Arty Bn	**115th RCT of 29th Inf Div**
5th ESB	4677th AAA Bn	115th Inf Regt
20th Engr Combat Bn	121st Engr Bn	110th Fd Arty Bn
81st CW Bn	6th ESB	
	112th Engr Combat Bn	**26th RCT of 1st Inf Div**
	81st CW Bn	26th Inf Regt
	461st Amphibious Truck Coy	33rd Fd Arty Bn

Battle Casualties, June 6–July 1, 1944

D-Day casualties are a matter of much debate and are not precise. However, what can be said is that of a total American armed forces death toll of 2,499 on that first day, around 2,000 were 1st and 29th Infantry Division soldiers. As an example, these are the Dagwood (16th Infantry) casualties identified at the National Archives:

	Officers	Enlisted Men
Killed in Action	5	45
Believed Killed in Action	10	26
Missing in Action	3	354
Wounded in Action	18	510
Total Regimental casualties	36	935

Of a total of 185 officers and 3,475 men, 149/2,538 were present for duty at the end of June 8 (the small discrepancy to the figures above is because of an inter-company movement).

Gordon Harrison (*United States Army in World War II: Cross-Channel Attack*) says that the V Corps losses for the day were about 2,000 killed, wounded, and missing. In a footnote, however, he adds: "This is frankly a guess, based on a number of estimates of various dates and various headquarters none of which agree. Under the Army's present casualty reporting system, it is unlikely that accurate figures of D-Day losses by unit will ever be available." The V Corps History gives D-Day losses as 2,374, of which the 1st Division lost 1,190, the 29th Division lost 743, and corps troops 441. The after action reports of the 1st Division and the 29th Division both scale down their own losses slightly. See Joseph H. Ewing, *29 Let's Go* (Washington 1948), p. 306. Source for the 1st Division report is its own G-1 report of daily casualties; source for the 29th Division figures is not given. On 8 June the 1st Division G-1 issued a "corrected" casualty report for D-Day and D+1 which reduced total losses reported for the two days from 1,870 to 1,036. (See V Corps G-3 Jnl.) Neither the original report nor the corrected one conforms to the division G-1's accounting in his monthly report of operations. See study of First Army casualties during June 1944, prepared by Royce L. Thompson, MS Hist Div files.

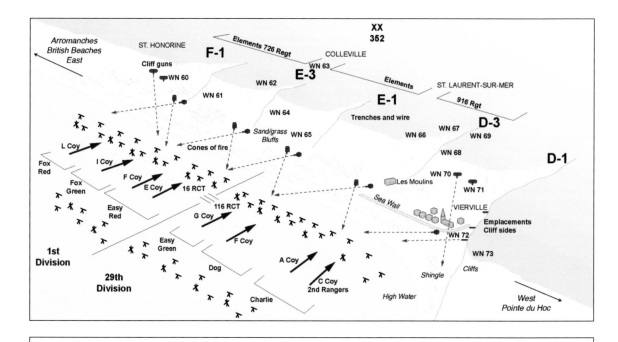

Above: German defensive strongpoints on Omaha.

WN 60
1 75mm gun
3 tobruks with mortars
1 mortar position
1 Flak 38 20mm gun
flamethrowers

WN 61
1 88mm Pak in pillbox
1 50mm Pak in concrete emplacement
1 tobruk with an R35 tank turret
2 tobruks with MGs flamethrowers

WN 62
2 75mm guns in pillboxes
2 50mm Pak guns
3 MG positions
1 tobruk with MG
2 tobruks with mortars
1 twin-AA MG in concrete
    emplacement
1 artillery observation post
    flamethrowers

WN 63
Company HQ
Radio station

WN 64
1 76.2mm gun
1 20mm Flak gun
2 tobruks with mortars

WN 65
1 50mm Pak in pillbox
1 50mm Pak in concrete emplacement
1 75mm gun
2 tobruks with mortars

WN 66
1 50mm Pak in concrete emplacement
1 AT gun
2 tobruks with tank turrets
2 heavy mortars in concrete
    emplacements
1 double-embrasure pillbox

WN 67
320mm rocket-launcher position

WN 68
1 50mm Pak in concrete emplacement
1 AT gun
2 tobruks with tank turrets
1 double-embrasure pillbox

WN 69
1 Flak gun
MG positions

WN 70
1 75mm gun in pillbox
1 75mm gun
4 tobruks with MGs
2 mortars in concrete emplacements
1 20mm Flak gun

WN 71
1 observation post
MG positions
1 tobruks with MG
1 mortar in concrete emplacement
1 double-embrasure pillbox

WN 72
1 88mm Pak in pillbox
1 50mm Pak double-embrasure pillbox
MG positions
1 tobruk with MG
1 double-embrasure pillbox

WN 73
1 75mm gun in pillbox
3 tobruks with mortars
MG positions
1 observation post

WN 74
2 75mm guns

Top, left and right: There were a number of antitank defenses along Omaha—minefields, dragon's teeth, antitank ditches and walls. Here, on June 8, men of 3204th QM Coy make their way past the wall at the bottom of Les Moulins draw: it had been dynamited on June 7.

Center left: The beach defenses may seem crude and haphazard, but they were effective on June 6. Many of them had Teller mines attached, which led to the destruction of a number of landing craft. Combined with the well-sited automatic weapons and enfilading heavier guns in their casemates, the defenders came within a whisker of seeing the attack off. In the end, the bravery of

the attacking troops, their numbers, and the naval support helped to contribute to the success of the landings—but at a great loss of life.

Center right: Fire trenches on the bluffs above the beach—these are part of *Widerstandsnest* (WN— resistance point) 68, on the western side of the D–3 draw.

Above: The biggest advantage for the defenders was the topography of the area—the shingle at the top of the beach and the high bluffs. However, the smoke raised by grass fires helped hide the attackers and gave some relief from the accurate machine-gun fire.

0 500 yds
0 500 m

1
2 3
5
4
6
7
8

Vierville-sur-Mer

D517 to seafront

D517

13

9
10

Les Moulins

11
12

La Fraisnaie

D30

Les Isles

D514 to Grandcamp-Maisy

17

Les Fossés Taillis

Vacqueville

Saint Laurent-sur-Mer

D194

D514

Above:
The area today is
studded with
memorials,
museums, and the
remains of German
casemates and
strongpoints.

Left:
Recon photo
showing the field
of battle.

Western beaches, 116th RCT

Eastern beaches, 16th RCT

D-1
Vierville

D-3
Les Moulins

E-1

E-3

F-1

St. Laurent-
sur-Mer

Colleville

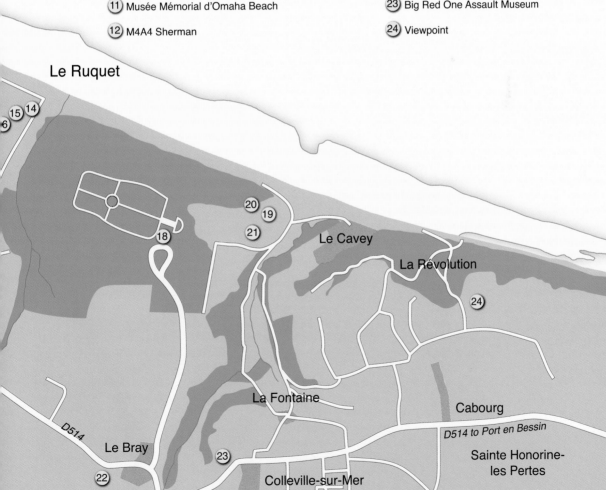

1. RAF 21 Base Defence Sector, 15082 GCI & Mobile Signals Unit Memorial
2. 58th Armored Field Battalion Memorial
3. National Guard Memorial
4. 6th Engineer Special Brigade Memorial
5. Memorial 29th American Infantry Division Omaha Beach
6. Section of Mulberry Harbour
7. Musée D-Day Omaha
8. 11th Port Plaque
9. Les Braves Memorial of Omaha Beach
10. Memorial Omaha Beach
11. Musée Mémorial d'Omaha Beach
12. M4A4 Sherman
13. Memorial First American War Cemetery in France
14. Pillbox 'Ruquet'
15. Memorial 2nd Infantry Division
16. Plaque 467th AAA Weapons Battalion
17. First Airstrip Monument
18. American Cemetery & Memorial
19. WN62 complex
20. Memorial 5th Engineer Special Brigade Omaha Beach
21. Big Red One Memorial
22. Overlord Museum
23. Big Red One Assault Museum
24. Viewpoint

Le Ruquet

Le Cavey

La Révolution

La Fontaine

Cabourg

D514

D514 to Port en Bessin

Le Bray

Colleville-sur-Mer

Sainte Honorine-les Pertes

Training

Below:
Stokenham was one of the villages mentioned on the memorial (opposite) and was damaged by shellfire.

Opposite, above:
An exercise on Slapton Sands. Photo shows Coast Guard-manned LCI(L)-85 which would be so severely damaged off Omaha by enemy fire that it sank.

Opposite, center:
Slapton Sands today and memorial of thanks to the inhabitants of the villages nearby who were evacuated to allow live firing exercises.

Opposite, below:
Map showing the location of places in England associated with 1st and 29th Infantry. Note Burton Bradstock and Slapton Sands.

THE FORCES THAT landed on Omaha were a mixture of seasoned troops—the 1st Inf Div, which had seen action in North Africa and Sicily in 1942 and 1943, and the yet unbloodied National Guardsmen of 29th Inf Div. When the Sicilian campaign was over, 1st Infantry returned to England to prepare for the invasion of Europe. Of the fighting in North Africa correspondent Ernie Pyle had said, "For you at home who think the African campaign was small stuff, let me tell you just this one thing—the First Division did more fighting then than it did throughout all of World War I." The fighting in Sicily was no less tough, and many in the division thought they had earned a trip home when that was over. Far from it, on October 23, 1943 they left Augusta, Sicily bound for England, arriving in Liverpool on November 5. Next came the train journey south to the county of Dorset, where the division was billeted in towns and villages from Bridport to Swanage, with headquarters in Dorchester.

The 29th Division had got there earlier. Part journeyed to England on September 27, 1942 on RMS *Queen Mary*; the rest followed on *Queen Elizabeth* the next week. The journey was far from uneventful. During the zigzagging they performed to protect against U-boat attack, *Queen Mary* collided with one of their escorts, HMS *Curacao*, an accident that left the cruiser sinking into the Atlantic. *Queen Mary* arrived in Greenock, Scotland, on October 3; *Elizabeth* on the 11th. The division then entrained for southern England, taking over Tidworth Camp from 1st Infantry which was Africa-bound. The 29th trained in Wiltshire until May 1943 when the division moved to the West Country, preparing for the invasion between Braunton and Barnstaple on the flat sandy beaches of the north Devon coast.

When 1st Inf Div returned to England, there followed six months of intensive training, including joint amphibious operations by both divisions at points on the south coast, particularly Slapton Sands, similar in terrain to Omaha. Operation Duck in December 1943/January 1944 was the first joint exercise.

In the middle of May 1944, the units left their training areas and moved closer to the coast and their embarkation points for Normandy: the 1st near Portland and Weymouth; the 29th Falmouth and Plymouth. Enclosed behind barbed wire, not allowed off camp, with camouflage the order of the day, it wasn't long before the men realized that training was over and their assault on Europe was imminent.

Wales

England

Oxford •

• Swansea

Newport •

London →

Cardiff •
Barry •

• Bristol

• Bath

Bristol Channel

Somerset

Tidworth Camp •

Barnstaple •

• Salisbury

Southampton •

Devon

Blandford
Forum •

Tarrant
Rushton
Airfield •

Portsmouth •

Upottery
Airfield •

Dunkeswell Airfield •

Maiden
Newton •

Dorset
Puddletown •

Bournemouth •

Okehampton •

Exeter Airfield •

Lyme Regis •

Exeter •

• Bridport

• Dorchester

Poole •

Burton Bradstock •

Swanage •

*Isle of
Wight*

Tavistock •

Lyme Bay

• Weymouth

Portland •

Bodmin Moor

Dartmoor

Teignmouth •

Torquay •

dmin •

Cornwall

Plymouth •

Dartmouth •

Slapton • • Slapton Sands

Fowey •

Stokenham •

Start Bay

English Channel

mouth •

THIS MEMORIAL
WAS PRESENTED BY THE
UNITED STATES ARMY
AUTHORITIES TO THE
PEOPLE OF THE SOUTH
HAMS WHO GENEROUSLY
LEFT THEIR HOMES AND
THEIR LANDS TO PROVIDE
A BATTLE PRACTICE AREA
FOR THE SUCCESSFUL
ASSAULT IN NORMANDY
IN JUNE 1944
THEIR ACTION RESULTED
IN THE SAVING OF MANY
HUNDREDS OF LIVES AND
CONTRIBUTED IN NO SMALL
MEASURE TO THE SUCCESS
OF THE OPERATION
THE AREA INCLUDED THE
VILLAGES OF BLACKAWTON
CHILLINGTON
EAST ALLINGTON SHERFORD
SLAPTON STOKENHAM
STRETE AND TORCROSS
TOGETHER WITH MANY
OUTLYING FARMS HOUSES

This page and opposite, below: Slapton witnessed a series of large-scale rehearsals for the D-Day landings, including Exercise Tiger, training the 4th Division that landed on Utah. On April 27, 1944, E-boats attacked and caused serious casualties, memorialized at Slapton by (**A**) an M4 pulled from the sea, and (**B**) the pillar on page 13.

Opposite, above and inset: To the east of Slapton Sands lie Blackpool Sands, overlooked from this vantage point on the road to Dartmouth. The children are watching an exercise below.

Dorset's planned contribution to D-Day changed on Sunday April 16, 1944, when the Allied High Command decided to relocate British invasion Force G (for Gold) eastwards to the harbors and inlets of the Solent and Southampton Water. Their place was taken by US Force O (for Omaha). The Supreme Commander, General Dwight D. Eisenhower, visited the main Dorset encampments, as did at least one photographer, whose article, "A Day in Burton Bradstock," used these images.

"It is estimated that a total of 80,000 American soldiers are now billetted in Dorset, from the chalets of Freshwater holiday camp on the coast at Burton Bradstock to Nissen huts in hazel coppices on Cranborne Chase."

This page:
"Four American soldiers sit in the sunshine on the pavement outside The Anchor Inn in Burton Bradstock and chat to local girl Betty 'Freckles' Mackay. According to the original caption, the nickname 'Freckles' was given to Betty by the GIs, who have 'made her a camp favourite'."

Left:

"Under the sycamore tree on the green at Burton Bradstock. Village children show off a machine gun belt washed up on Chesil Beach to GI's John L. Lawson of Port Jervis, New York, Robert S. Hastings of Azusa, California, Leo H. Pearson of Springfield, New York and Corporal Roland Henry of Holland, Pennsylvania."

Left:

Burton Bradstock housed the Big Red One for two months before the invasion. This is Red House Garage in April 1944. Behind the thatched cottage is the village playing field with the church tower in the distance. The presence of a "Headquarters" vehicle shows the importance of this photographic session.

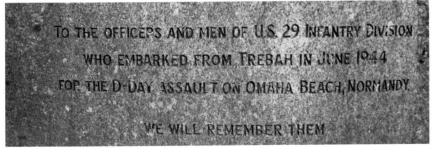

Below:

Plaque remembering 29th Infantry Division's stay at Tavistock. HQ was based at Abbotsfield Hall, today a nursing home.

Below, left:

Trebah Gardens remembers the 29th Division. *Vernon39*

TO THE OFFICERS AND MEN OF U.S. 29 INFANTRY DIVISION
WHO EMBARKED FROM TREBAH IN JUNE 1944
FOR THE D-DAY ASSAULT ON OMAHA BEACH, NORMANDY.

WE WILL REMEMBER THEM

Into Battle

Weymouth was one of the main embarkation points for troops marshaled in South Dorset—mainly the 1st Division. The 29th Division staged through Cornwall, particularly Falmouth and Helston. The marshaling areas were often known as "sausage camps" because of the way they were identified on maps. Concealed as far as possible from aerial surveillance, they often had temporary accommodations, sometimes just tents. There were also several hospitals in Weymouth to receive casualties who were evacuated from Normandy.

	1st wave intended	1st wave actual	2nd wave intended	2nd wave actual
RCT 116: 29th Infantry Division/743rd Tk Bn				
Charlie				
	C/2 Rangers (ele)	C/2 Rangers (ele)		B/116 ele
Dog Green				
	A/116	A/116	5 Rangers (-) C/116 D/116 B/116	D/116 B/116 ele A and B/2 Rangers
Dog White				
	G/116		K/116 H/116 (ele)	C/116 B/2 Rangers C/5 Rangers 29th Division assistant commander BG Dutch Cota
Dog Red				
	F/116	F/116	M/116 I/116 H/116 (ele)	B/5 Rangers H/116 I/116
Easy Green				
	E/116		H/116 (ele) L/116	K/116 L/116 (ele)
		G/116		
RCT16: 1st Inf Div/741st Tk Bn				
Easy Red				
	E/16		I/16	L/116 (ele)
	F/16		H/16	M/116
		E/116 ele	G/16	A-B/16
		E/16 ele		G/16
				C/16
				D/16
				H/16 (ele)
Fox Green				
	I/16		M/16	H/16 (ele)
	L/16		K/16	K/16
		E/116 ele		M/16
		E/16 (-)		I(-)/16 (from first wave)
		F/116 (-)		
Fox Red				
		L/16		

This spread:
Weymouth harbor has changed little over the years as the today photo (**Left**) shows.

Opposite, below:
The actual arrival of units onto Omaha Beach was very different to that intended.

Opposite:
The 1st Division prepares to sail for Normandy. The insignia of the Big Red One can be seen on almost all of the soldiers' helmets, and also on their left shoulder. All these men wear the battle dress with wool trousers and M1941 combat jacket or tanker jacket.

Above:
Boarding ships in Weymouth Harbor. In front of the LCAs are US Rangers in *LCI(L)-497, -84 and LCH-87*. On the dock is a member of the Signal Corps with his camera in hand. Weymouth Pavilion is behind the photographer.

Left:
A memorial on Weymouth Esplanade is dedicated to the American soldiers who embarked through the town.

Above:

Medical Jeep of the 5th BSE embarks on its LCT at Portland Harbor. The row of houses opposite show the image to be at Castletown in a row still standing today.

Below:

In the background LST-134 loads vehicles attached to the HQ element of US 1st Infantry Division bound for Easy Red, Omaha Beach. It was part of Task Force 124.5 (Assault Group 0-3) and was to land units of the 18th RCT on the beaches of Fox Green and Easy Red (eastern sector of Omaha Beach) June 6, 1944. This is part of LST Group 30 of the LST Flotilla 12.

Above:
The assault wave left their transports and scrambled down the side netting to their attack craft around 03:00–03:30. These had been dropped into the sea from davits with their boat team. All had loaded by 04:15.

Left:
Men of the 29th Division wait on their transport. The photograph shows well the equipment carried by men on D-Day. Note waterproofed rifles, life preservers, and the rubberized M5 waterproofed gasmask haversack on the top of the chest.

The Assault

1 Second-wave landing craft carrying 1/16th Inf Regt approach Easy Red, around 07:15.

2 and 3 Robert F. Sargent, USCG, took these photos from an LCVP carrying men of 1st Infantry from USS *Samuel*. The time is 07:30 and the craft beaches near the Ruquet draw (E–1). A tank is visible on the beach.

4 An 18th Infantry landing craft nears the beach, following a DUKW.

Hᴏᴡ ᴍᴀɴʏ ᴛɪᴍᴇꜱ have you read the phrase "Bloody Omaha"? Today, as you look out over the peaceful sands it's hard to believe that so much blood was spilt here—American and German. Occupied by the 726th and 916th Regiments of 352th Inf Div, who had practiced their defense, ranged their weapons and were safely hidden in carefully sited trenches and bunkers, it was on Omaha Beach that the Atlantic Wall in Normandy was at its strongest.

As could be expected, the first wave took the brunt of it: the 24 LCVPs of the 116th RCT of the 29th Inf Div in particular, as they landed in front of the heavily defended western end of the beach. The defenders had been roughed up by the pre-invasion bombardment, but most bombs had been dropped too far from the coast and the rockets launched from the sea had also overshot. Carrying around 30 men each, the LVCPs opened their ramps onto the expanse of beach and the infantry charged: a full frontal attack into a killing zone enfiladed from each side, with machine guns opening up in front of them and artillery and mortar batteries laying down an intensive barrage.

It was murder. Those craft that reached the shore disgorged their men into hell. Many were hit immediately. Those that weren't tried to hide under the water or behind beach obstacles, advancing up the beach with the tide. All cohesion and military order went out the window. The worst affected was Dog Green (see map on page 5) where A Company, 1st Battalion, 116th Infantry, from the Virginia National Guard in Bedford, VA was almost wiped out.

Then the second wave came in. Seeing what had happened to the earlier boats, many of the LVCPs tried to find safety by landing further east, causing chaos. Delivery of vital equipment, too, suffered. The combat engineers lost their markers and couldn't identify channels cleared of mines. Artillery and armor didn't reach the beach. The army depended on its communications, but radios were in short supply: in *Cross Channel Attack* Gordon Harrison notes that three-quarters of the 116th Infantry's radios were destroyed or useless. In a footnote he relates, "Five men of the 16th Infantry were decorated for their heroic work in struggling ashore with vital radios and wire despite serious wounds. T/5 John J. Pinder, Jr., received a posthumous award of the Medal of Honor for his intrepidity in recovering two radios and other equipment, while suffering two severe wounds. On his third trip into the fire-swept surf he was killed."

However, slowly, small groups of men managed to infiltrate the bluffs—generally thanks to landing away from the direct fire of a *Widerstandsnest*, or where the fog of war and smoke from fires helped obscure them from the Germans. Around Les Moulins draw, urged on by Gen. "Dutch" Cota, the 5th Rangers led the way with small groups of 116th Infantry. Elsewhere, 16th Infantry infiltrated between St. Laurent and Colleville. Aided by the surviving tanks on the beach and by the supporting fire from destroyers which approached close enough to ground, the deadlock was broken. The battle for the beach moved into the hinterland.

Today, on the bluffs once held by the German defenders, sits the American cemetery at Colleville, laid out in an area of 170 acres ceded to the United States by the French government. A new visitor center explains what happened on the beach below. Outside, the cemetery contains 9,387 gravestones. Every day at 16:30, visitors can watch the ceremony of the Lowering of the Colors. To the sound of a military hymn, the American flag is lowered and folded.

5 Smoke obscures the beach: at sea, Bradley contemplated pulling out of Omaha.

6 "Naval Demolition Men Blowing Up Obstacles," an ink and wash artwork by Mitchell Jamieson. The NCDUs (Navy Combat Demolition Units) were scheduled to blow 16 50-foot-wide gaps through the beach obstacles for the follow-up infantry waves. This turned out to be a near suicidal role as many of the teams were hit as they brought their demolition equipment to the obstacles. Six gaps—one each at Dog White and Easy Green, the other four at Easy Red—were eventually cleared by engineers and demolition crews who sustained casualties of over 40%.

25

Above:
"The Battle for Fox Green Beach." This watercolor by Navy Combat Artist Dwight Shepler, 1944, shows USS *Emmons* (DD-457) bombarding in support of the landings. There is no doubt that supporting naval gunfire, particularly from the destroyers that got close enough to shore to scrape on the bottom, tipped the balance on Omaha. "Without that gunfire we positively could not have crossed the beaches," said Col. S.B. Mason of 1st Division.

Below:
"The Tough Beach." Watercolor by Navy Combat Artist Dwight Shepler, showing German artillery fire hitting USS *LCI(L)-93*, aground and holed. More Coast Guard vessels were lost or damaged that day than at any time in its history. Destroyed in action were *LCI(L)-85*, *-91*, *-92*, and *-93*, as well as over 20 LCVPs and 4 LCTs.

Left:
M4s loaded in an LCT ready for the invasion. Note the extended air intakes for operations in water.

Below, left:
Knocked-out vehicles cover Dog Red Beach west of Les Moulins, after the assault on the beach. This tank, named *Ceaseless* by its crew, is from C Coy 743rd Tank Battalion.

Below, right:
Scene on Omaha Beach on the afternoon of D-Day, showing casualties on the beach, a bogged-down Sherman tank, several wrecked trucks and German anti-landing obstructions.

The armor supporting the landings was made up of the 743rd (RCT 116 to the west) and 741st (RCT 16 east) Tank Battalions, each with 48 tanks of which 32 were DD (Duplex Drive) equipped and eight tank dozers. Both units would win Presidential Unit Citations for their actions on D-Day. The 743rd fared better than the 741st, 27 of whose DD tanks foundered in the 6ft waves and sank before reaching the shore—some as close as 1,000m from land. Only two, skippered by commanders with small-boat experience, successfully crossed the 6,000 yards of choppy sea from the launching. Three others were delivered intact to shore by *LCT-600*. The follow-up of M4A1s equipped with wading equipment landed directly brought the 741st's total to 18. By the end of the day, they could muster only three. The naval commander of the 743rd, however, did not launch its DDs, preferring to take them direct to shore. 40 of the 48 landed safely on Dog Green and Dog Red, four having been lost with the company CO when the LCT was sunk; four others were knocked out. This meant that 58 of 96 tanks reached the beaches, but they found the incoming tide and stony shingle difficult to negotiate and so were hampered in action. Nine DSCs were awarded to men of the 743rd for actions on June 6, 1944.

Vierville (D-1)

1 The road from Vierville (**A**) down Draw D–1. At **B** a length of Mulberry roadway; **C** 6th ESB Memorial; **D** 29th Inf Div Memorial; **E** WN71 MG embrasures; **F** WN72; **G** Mulberry caisson; **H** WN73 bunker.

2 Diagram showing the key features of WN72 and WN71 (green = trenches; purple = wire): 1 Antitank ditch; 2 Antitank barrier; 3 Embrasures for two MGs; 4 Mortar pit; 5 Bunker for a 50mm PAK38; 6 MG Tobruk; 7 Antitank wall; 8 677 bunker for a 88mm PAK43; 9 Hotel; 10 Embrasures in cliff; 11 MG position; 12 Tobruks for mortar.

3 and 4 WN73 on the high ground west of WN72 included a bunker for a 75mm. It enfiladed the western end of the beach.

5

6

7

5 WN71 included two embrasures that covered the D–1 draw.

6 The 29th Infantry memorial, a granite obelisk, was raised for the 50th anniversary of D-Day. The inscription on the front is in English and French; on the sides are listed the specific battalions, units and platoons which comprised the division on that day. On the back of the obelisk are the campaigns in which the 29th participated as well as the number of casualties the unit sustained. "From north and south in our land we came that freedom might prevail. On D-Day, June 6 1944, in the great Allied amphibious assault, the 29th Infantry Division stormed ashore on Omaha Beach to win a beachhead. Our fallen lie among you. They gave the last full measure of their devotion. Sleep, comrades, forever young. We salute you."

7 Memorial to the 6th ESB: "The fight for the first thousand yards," In Memoriam to all members of this command who lived, fought and died for the cause of freedom.

8 and 9 Looking from WN72 toward the west end of Omaha Beach. Note the substantial shingle bank—there is little of this left on Omaha today because it was used to fill in the antitank ditches and provide hard core for roads. It was here that the Rangers scaled the cliffs.

8

9

1–3 WN72 casemates then and now. Today, WN72 is surmounted by the National Guard Monument, and "sits on the spot where the 29th National Guard Division broke through German defenses on D-Day, June 6, 1944. The monument and the original bunker which it sits atop are maintained by NGEF to preserve the legacy and pay honor to all National Guardsmen who have fought in the European theater."

4 View from the 677 bunker.

5 View from WN73 over the WN72 casemates.

6–8 The 677 bunker has the 88mm PAK43 that defended D–1 draw still in place. The casemate behind had a double embrasure and a Ringstand allowing its 50mm Kwk to fire to east and west. No longer visible are the MG positions and the antitank wall that blocked the draw until it was finally blown by engineers after the pillbox had been knocked out.

9 WN71, on the other side of D–1, seen from WN72.

10 116th Regimental Combat Team statue. Nearby a plaque reads "Ever Forward; In commemoration of the determined effort by the soldiers of the 29th Division's 116th Infantry Regimental Combat Team who landed the morning of June 6, 1944 on this section of Omaha Beach, known as Exit D–1, to open the Vierville Draw behind you to begin the liberation of Europe."

11 Memorial to the 58th Armored Field Artillery Battalion.

6

7

8

9

10

11

Right:

April 1944 photo of Vierville area showing: **A** Draw D–1; **B** the probable location that Lt. Taylor left the beach; **C** the Manoir de Than; **D** Vierville church; **E** Ormel farm.

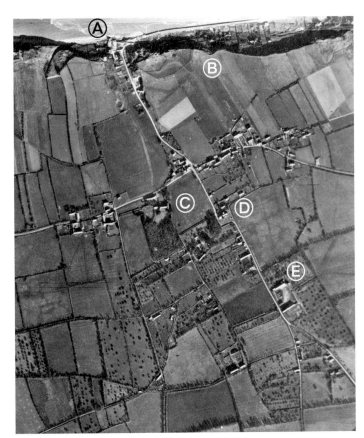

Below:

By the time it reached the shore, B Coy 1/116 Infantry Regt was commanded by 2-Lt. Walter P. Taylor, the senior officers having been killed during the assault. Taylor, almost miraculously, led his men off the beach and reached Ormel farm where they fought until sundown, joined by a small band of Rangers. Taylor was awarded the DSC "for extraordinary heroism in connection with military operations against an armed enemy while serving with the 116th Infantry Regiment, 29th Infantry Division, in action against enemy forces on 6 June 1944. Second Lieutenant Taylor's intrepid actions, personal bravery and zealous devotion to duty exemplify the highest traditions of the military forces of the United States and reflect great credit upon himself, the 29th Infantry Division, and the United States Army."

Left:
A tower of the château of Vierville that was probably hit by a five-inch shell from USS *Texas* towards 06:00 on the morning of June 6.

Below:
The church at Vierville, as so many in Normandy, lost its tower and spire in the fighting.

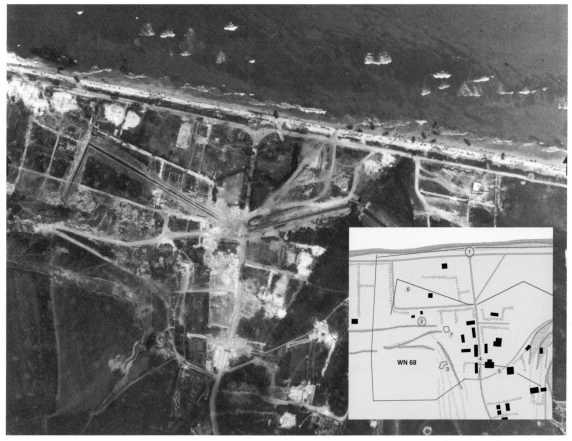

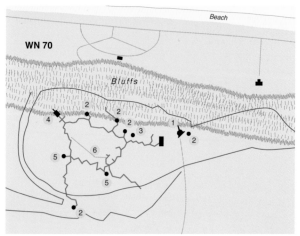

Les Moulins (D-3)

Above:

WN68 lay to the west of the D–3 Les Moulins draw, 66 was in the center and WN67 on the eastern bluff (see p. 36). Today (**Below right**) the layout is very different, and there is little sign of the defenses. The inset diagram shows WN68: **1** 50mm KwK position; **2** VK3001 75mm KwK tank turret (**Opposite, center right**); **3** Double embrasure MG position; **4** Entrance (closed at night); **5** Antitank wall; **6** Blue line identifies water-filled antitank ditch; **7** 667 bunker under construction. There were other MG positions among the trenches on the bluffs.

Left and below left:

Between Vierville (D-1) and Les Moulins (D-3), WN70 was on the bluffs. This drawing identifies: **1** 612 75mm bunker under construction (also Below left); **2** Hardened MG positions; **3** 20mm Flak 30; **4** 80mm FK17(t); **5** 80mm mortar pits; **6** Underground passageway.

Above left and right:
Les Sables d'Or, one of the few houses left standing in the area, is where Maj. Sidney Bingham, CO 1/116th Inf Regt, 29th Division, landed. The citation for his DSC reads: "Pinned down on the beach by the heavy and intense enemy fire, Maj. Bingham gathered together five of his men and personally led them across the beach and up a cliff in an attempt to seek out an enemy machine gun that had been inflicting heavy casualties on his unit. Though unable to reach the machine gun, he was, nevertheless, able to discover its location. He returned to the fire-swept beach and organized a flank and rear attack which succeeded in taking the enemy position, thereby permitting his unit to advance." Today there is no sign of the house or the shingle.

Center left:
VK3001 75mm KwK tank turret, one of six prototypes for a tank that didn't enter production. A number were used in the defense of Omaha.

Left:
Aerial view looking over WN68 toward WN66 (seafront). The D-3 draw today is the site of two important monuments: **A** The Liberation (see p. 36); **B** "Les Braves" (see p. 37).

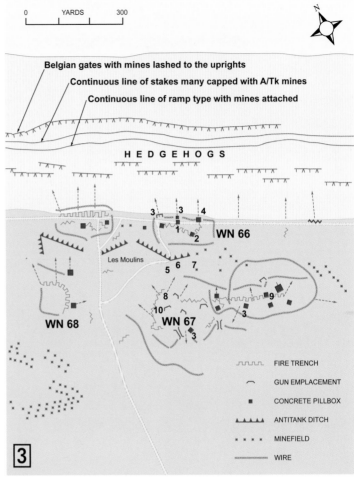

Belgian gates with mines lashed to the uprights

Continuous line of stakes many capped with A/Tk mines

Continuous line of ramp type with mines attached

H E D G E H O G S

0   YARDS   300

WN 66

Les Moulins

WN 68

WN 67

	FIRE TRENCH
	GUN EMPLACEMENT
■	CONCRETE PILLBOX
▲▲▲	ANTITANK DITCH
• • • •	MINEFIELD
~~	WIRE

1 The Liberation, 1st Division, and 116th RCT monument has inscriptions on the sides dedicated to the Big Red One and to the 116th RCT of the 29th Div (see p.35).

2 M4AT Outside the Musée Mémorial d'Omaha Beach—it's not a WW2 vehicle. The T stands for *Transforme*. It was supplied to the French Army in 1952 and upgraded.

3 Taken from a US plan, this diagram shows the range of defenses, including three of the four WNs, protecting D–3 draw—none visible today. Not shown here, WN69 was a Nebelwerfer unit in St Laurent itself. Note: 1 Sables d'Or house (see p.35); 2 Barracks; 3 MG position; 4 50mm KwK position; 5 612 bunker under construction; 6 50mm KwK position and Tobruk for a VK3001 turret (see p. 35); 7 677 bunker under construction; 8 Tobruk R35 37mm KwK 144(f); 9 Two 81mm mortar pits; 10 Double embrasure MG position.

4 The trenches of WN67 on the bluff above the beach. The photo shows the lack of vegetation that now clads the area.

5 "Les Braves" by artist Anilore Banon is a more recent sculpture (dating from 2004) in memory of the bravery of those who fought on the beach.

6 Construction was underway on these two bunkers (6 on diagram) when it was halted by the invasion.

7 Two other bunkers were under construction, a 677 and a 612.

Le Ruquet (E–1)

Above:

The water-filled antitank ditch that defended Le Ruquet draw is at the top of this photo taken c. 12:00 on June 6. It was on the beach that "Pvt. Barrett, landing in the face of extremely heavy enemy fire, was forced to wade ashore through neck-deep water. Disregarding the personal danger, he returned to the surf again and again to assist his floundering comrades and save them from drowning … [Barrett] working with fierce determination, saved many lives by carrying casualties to an evacuation boat lying offshore." Carlton W. Barrett of 18th Inf Regt received the Congressional Medal of Honor for his bravery.

Below:

The E-1 draw today. The bunker is identified at A; the 2nd Inf Div memorial (see p. 40) at B.

Inset:

WN65 showing **1** 667 bunker with 50mm PAK38; **2** Another 667 under construction; **3** MG positions; **4** 50mm KwK position; **5** Villa l'Abri Côtier; **6** 75mm PAK40; **7** 50mm PAK38; **8** Mortar Tobruk

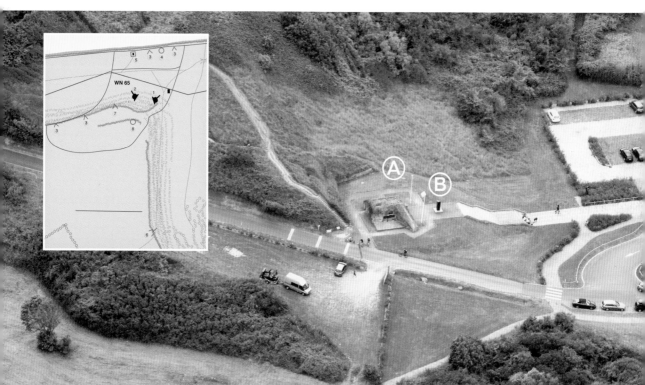

Left and below left:
The Provisional Engineer Special Group used the 667 bunker as a HQ and their exploits readying the beach for troop movements were remembered in the first plaque to be placed on the bunker.

Below:
This 50mm antitank gun in the Type 677 casemate proved to be one of the most effective elements of the WN65 strongpoint covering the E-1 St Laurent draw. It was finally silenced by 37mm automatic cannon fire from a pair of M15A1 multiple gun motor carriage halftracks of the 467th AAA Battalion. Today it has a plaque honoring that unit (visible **top**). The nearby interpretive plaque reads: "At Ruquet, 6 June, the first open road to the interior. On 6 June, at around 10am, hundreds of men were stuck on this beach amongst the destroyed landing crafts. In front of them was the small Ruquet valley, protected by two fortified points. Today, all that is visible is one large gun in its blockhouse. It was hit by fire from an approaching vessel 1km (1,000 yards) away, and was destroyed for good by a 'half-track'. The U.S. Engineers immediately opened this road towards the plateau, and at around 3pm, the heavy U.S. equipment took this first, and only, cleared exit from the Omaha site."

There were many acts of bravery in the surf of Omaha on June 6, and three men were awarded the Congressional Medal of Honor for their actions. One of them was baseball star T/5 Joe Pinder, "the stocky, square-set little Pennsylvanian with the blinding fastball." He landed "under devastating enemy machinegun and artillery fire which caused severe casualties among the boatload. Carrying a vitally important radio, he struggled towards shore in waist-deep water. Only a few yards from his craft he was hit by enemy fire and was gravely wounded. T/5 Pinder never stopped. He made shore and delivered the radio. Refusing to take cover afforded, or to accept medical attention for his wounds, T/5 Pinder, though terribly weakened by loss of blood and in fierce pain, on 3 occasions went into the fire-swept surf to salvage communication equipment. He recovered many vital parts and equipment, including another workable radio … Remaining exposed to heavy enemy fire, growing steadily weaker, he aided in establishing the vital radio communication on the beach. While so engaged this dauntless soldier was hit for the third time and killed."

Top:
2nd Infantry Division Memorial.

Above and below:
The follow-up troops of 2nd Inf Div move past the bunker on June 7.

The first wave had foundered; the second wave was equally hard-pressed. As the tide came in, the beach shrank; equipment was submerged; the wounded drowned. But although those trapped on the shingle thought all hope was gone, slowly the tactical position changed. Helped by accurate naval gunfire, slowly small groups infiltrated the bluffs. 3/116th RCT supported by the heavy weapons of M/116 reached the top between D–3 and E–1. Between E–1 and E–3 it was elements of G/16, E/16, and E/116. One by one the *Widerstandsnester* were taken. An example of these acts of heroism, 2-Lt. John M. Spalding of the Big Red One's 16th Inf Regt was awarded the DSC. His citation reads: "Spalding led his men in the attack on a series of enemy strongpoints and successfully destroyed them. Constantly ignoring heavy enemy fire, he at all times continued in the advance and personally destroyed an antitank gun which had been firing on beach targets with deadly effect."

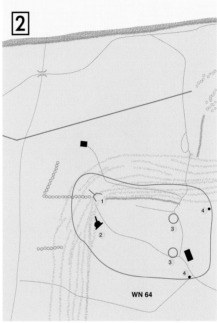

Far left:
WN64 on the east side of the Le Ruquet valley, was a weak point. The 612 bunker was incomplete and the 76mm IKH 290(r) visible at bottom right of this photo fought from an open emplacement.

Left: WN64 consisted of: **1** 76mm gun; **2** Bunker under construction; **3** Two mortar pits; **4** Two MG Tobruks. Note the water-filled antitank ditch (blue line).

Left:
The view over the 612 bunker under construction showing its field of fire over the beach looking toward WN65. WN64 was taken by 2–Lt John M. Spalding who received the DSC for his bravery.

WN 64

41

Right and below right:
The road leading down the E–3 Colleville draw. It was defended by WNs 60, 61, and 62.

Bottom right:
LCI(L)-490 and *LCI(L)-496* try to find a cleared channel to Fox Green beach.

Opposite, above:
E-3 draw today, highlighting: **A** WN62 and The Big Red One memorial (also shown on page 44) which stands just above the largest defensive position on Omaha, sited some 100ft above the beach. It was manned by men of the 716th and 352nd Inf Divs, and artillery observers from a battery of 105mm artillery inland at Houtteville. Among its personnel was Gefreiter Heinrich Severloh—the "Beast of Omaha"—whose biography talked of him firing over 12,000 rounds, killing hundreds. **B** WN62 included two 669 casemates, the view of the beach from one is shown (**opposite, center right**). Today the 5th ESB memorial is placed on top of this bunker (see p. 44). There are also plaques for the 299th, 146th, and the 20th Engineer Combat Bns, and lower down, for Canadian Navy minesweepers. **C** The other 669. **D** US cemetery at Colleville; **E** WN61 on west side of draw; **F** The start of the cliffs visible in many photos of Fox Red landings is to the east (left).

Opposite, center left:
This is the 50mm gun commanded by Gefreiter Siegfried Kuska in strongpoint WN62 that covered the entrance to the Colleville draw. It was emplaced in an ordinary field entrenchment.

Opposite, bottom:
120mm mortars of 81st Chemical Battalion lay down fire on WN62 from WN61.

Colleville (E-3)

Right:
The Big Red One memorial. Monuments of the same design can be found at Mons, Henri-Chapelle and Butgenbach in Belgium and Cheb in the Czech Republic. They follow the path of the Big Red One through the war.

Far right and below:
The 5th ESB memorial sits on top of one of two 669 bunkers that enfiladed the beach (**A and B below**), with 75mm FK 235(f) field guns. Note the artillery observation post at **C**. Just down the bluff from the American cemetery and visitor center and Big Red One memorials, this site gives a good impression of the fields of fire available to the Germans.

WN62 was surrounded by wire; there was an antitank ditch to the west and another water-filled ditch 5 feet deep and 7 feet wide stretching across the draw. At its eastern end there were remote-controlled flamethrowers. Other features included: **1** Type 669 bunkers; **2** Antitank guns—fixed 50mm KwK near sea (see photo p. 43); mobile 75mm PAK40 higher up; **3** Artillery observation post for 1st Bty Regt 352 at Houtteville; **4** Communications room; **5** Optical messaging post to ensure contact was maintained with WNs 61 and 63; **6** 50mm mortar Tobruks (also **D1** and **D2** on photo opposite); **7** Water-tank; **8** MG positions; **9** Bunkers to shelter men and ammunition; **10** House used as canteen etc; **11** Entrances to the position; **12** Organization Todt railway taking building materials to WN61; **13** Firing platforms for field guns (unused); **14** 667 bunker under construction.

La Révolution (F–1)

WN61 (at the right end of the antitank ditch—see photo p.45), protecting the F–1 draw up to La Revolution valley, boasted a 677 bunker (**1 and 2**) housing an 88mm PAK43/41 (**6**) seen here out of sits bunker; a number of MG including this Tobruk (**3**); a 50cm KwK on a pedestal mounting (see **5**); two mortar pits; a 50mm Tobruk; and a R35 37mm KwK turret.

4 View over the position from the east. Landing at 06:30, the 16/1st Infantry suffered very heavy losses. They took cover on the pebble bank out of line-of-sight of the German machine guns, but they were harassed by mortar and artillery shells. Hardly visible in the undergrowth, this photo shows the rear of the blockhouse that contained one of only two 88mm antitank guns on Omaha Beach. SSgt Turner Sheppard's M4 of 741st Tank Bn managed to destroy it by 07:10. In one of only two DD tanks to reach shore, Sheppard's luck ran out that afternoon on the road to Colleville. He had exited the beach via E–1 at around 17:00, leading infantry up the draw and was knocked out by an antitank gun.
7 View from above WN61. It was taken before the storm of June 19–21.

1 Renault tank turret embedded at WN60.

2, 3, and 4 Today, the position still gives an excellent view of the beach, and the mortar positions are still there. **1** Two 75mm 235(b), field guns in open positions; **2** Artillery observation post; **3** Tobruks with mortars; **4** Renault R35 turret with 37mm gun, **5** MG positions; **6** Mortar and machine gun Tobruk; **7** Shelters, a number linked by underground passages.

5 Looking west from WN60, at the eastern extreme of Omaha Beach, around June 10. **A** is E–3 draw; **B** is the line of ships forming the Gooseberry between Les Moulins (D–3) and E–3; **C** is F–1 Draw.

6 The cliffs allowed troops to leave the landing craft out of sight of the German defenses.

7 Back for more! LST-603 launched four DD Shermans from B/741st Tank Bn and later returned, this time to Fox Green, to land jeeps from 18th Div and 32nd Fd Arty.

8, 9, and 10 Elements of 16th Inf Regt, 1st Infantry Division (**8**) make their way to F–1 draw under cover of the cliffs (**9 & 10**).

The east end of Omaha is recognizable for its cliffs (**Opposite**), and four sections of L/16th Inf Regt landed there rather than on Fox Green because of the current. Above was WN60 with a brilliant position looking down Omaha, protected by minefields, barbed wire, and 40 men. However, its defensive qualities weren't as good as those further down the beach and it was the first strongpoint to be taken on June 6. Reinforced by elements of I/16, K/16 and E/116, the American troops found a path that led behind it and were able to attack from the rear. By 09:00 it had been taken and 3rd Bn 16th RCT was able to move inland.

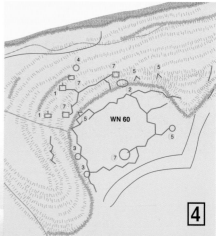

6

7

8

9

10

Ste. Honorine des Pertes

Opposite:
Until PLUTO—the pipeline under the ocean from UK to France—could be set up, Ste Honorine des Pertes, to the east of Omaha, and Port en Bessin were chosen as the arrival points for fuel which was pumped to a collection point at Êtréham.

Left and below left:
Aerial views of Ste. Honorine.

Below and bottom right:
Êtréham was where the fuel dump was set up. The village was liberated as the Big Red One moved inland on June 7.

Bottom left:
The pipeline comes ashore.

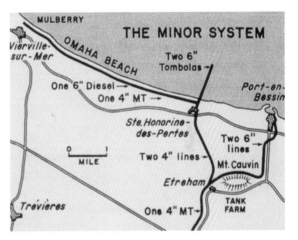

51

Advancing Inland

Opposite, above:
The church at
Colleville was
destroyed by a naval
shell on June 6.

Opposite, center:
Men of 2nd Inf Div
pass the town hall
around June 8.

Opposite, below:
The latest major
museum in the Omaha
hinterland is situated
on the D514
roundabout that
provides access to the
American Cemetery at
Colleville-sur-Mer. It
has a number of
armored vehicles out
front—this an
M4A1(76mm).

Top:
An M4A1 of the 741st
Tank Bn has made it to
Colleville.

Above left and left:
A DUKW turns off
the sea road.

Left and Below Left:
Formigny, Church of St. Martin. The main advance from the beaches was made by follow-up troops—the 18th Inf Regt, with the 3/26th Inf Regt attached, south and south-eastwards. The heaviest opposition was encountered at Formigny where troops of the 2/915th Grenadiers had reinforced 2/916th Grenadiers. Attempts by 3/26 and B/18 with support from the tanks of B/745 were held off and the town did not fall until the morning of June 8.

Right and Below:
Trevières was strongly defended. After a heavy artillery barrage, a platoon got inside the town but was held up by sniper and automatic weapons fire until third battalion waded the river, and attacked from the west flank of the town. So tenacious was the German grip that the objective was not entirely outflanked and secured until the next day. A and B show location of then and now photos.

Mulberry

Each of the two artificial Mulberry harbors was made up of about 6 miles of flexible steel roadways that floated on steel or concrete pontoons. The roadways were codenamed "Whales" and the pontoons "Beetles." The "Whales" ended at giant pier heads that had "legs" that rested on the seabed. The whole structure was protected from the force of the sea by scuttled ships, sunken caissons (one of which is at Vierville: see photo **Below**) and a line of floating breakwaters. The material requirements for any part of either Mulberry A or B were huge—144,000 tons of concrete, 85,000 tons of ballast and 105,000 tons of steel.

Above:
Mulberry A before the storm. Constructed by Seebees of the 108th Construction Bn, the gooseberry was completed by D+4, as was the first whale roadway. By D+12, over 310,000 men had reached France, many of them via this mulberry.

Right:
Mulberry A was constructed at Omaha Beach capable of moving 7,000 tons of vehicles and goods each day. This is part of the preserved section on the road to Vierville (see p.28).

Opposite: In the early morning of July 19 the winds got up and waves of 12ft were experienced. Vessels were ripped from their moorings and hit the structure, damaging it seriously—as can be seen in these June 21 photos. Mulberry A was never rebuilt.

The map labels:

Depth 6m
Depth 12m
Floating breakwaters
20 Phoenix caisson breakwaters
7 Phoenix
4 Phoenix
Floating bridgeways
Floating docks
3 Phoenix
Battleship HMS *Centurion* scuttled
13 old merchant ships scuttled
Low tide
High tide
D-1
Vierville
Sector Dog
Causeway
D-3
St Laurent
Sector Easy
E-1
Le Ruquet
Causeway
E-3
Sector Fox
Colleville

0   1000 yards
0   1000 m

The First Airstrip

Left:
Advanced Landing Ground A-1 was one of the first established airfields in the liberated area of Normandy, constructed by the IX Engineering Command, 834th Engineer Aviation Bn. Construction of the airfield began on June 7 on the bluffs above Omaha Beach, and was completed on June 8 at 18:00. Today there is memorial marking the spot.

The First Cemetery

The first American Cemetery at Omaha was on the foreshore and is identified today by a memorial at **A** in photo below.

Normandy American Cemetery and Memorial

The Normandy American Cemetery and Memorial is a tranquil place today with an excellent museum. Amongst those buried here is Lt. Jimmy Monteith of 16th Inf Regt, 1st Infantry. The citation for his Congressional Medal of Honor relates how he landed with the initial assault waves and, under heavy enemy fire without regard to his own personal safety led his men to the comparative safety of a cliff. Retracing his steps to the beach, he moved to where 2 tanks were buttoned up and blind under violent enemy artillery and machinegun fire. Completely exposed to the intense fire, he led the tanks on foot through a minefield and into firing positions. Under his direction several enemy positions were destroyed. Supervising the defense of his newly won position against repeated vicious counterattacks, when the enemy succeeded in surrounding him and his unit and while leading the fight out of the situation, Monteith was killed by enemy fire.

JIMMIE W. MONTEITH JR
1 LT 16 INF 1 DIV
VIRGINIA JUNE 6 1944
MEDAL OF HONOR

AMERICAN BATTLE MONUMENTS COMMISSION

Normandy American Cemetery
and Memorial

WWW.ABMC.GOV

Bibliography

Balkoski, Joseph: *Beyond the Beachhead The 29th Infantry Division in Normandy*; Stackpole Books, 1989.

Balkoski, Joseph: *Omaha Beach D-Day*; Stackpole Books, 2004.

Bernage, Georges: *Omaha Beach*; Heimdal, 2002.

Férey, Emmanuel: *Atlantikwall Omaha Beach*; Editions Histoire & Fortifications, 2014.

Harrison, Gordon A.: *US Army in WW2 The European Theater of Operations Cross-Channel Attack*; CMH, US Army, Washington, D.C., 2002.

Kershaw, Robert J.: *D-Day Piercing the Atlantic Wall*; Ian Allan, 1993.

Mayo, Jonathan: *D-Day Minute-by-Minute*; Short Books, 2014.

Ramsey, Winston G. [Ed]: *D-Day Then and Now* (two vols); After the Battle, 1995.

Whitlock, Flint: *The Fighting First The Untold Story of the Big Red One on D-Day*; Westview Press, 2004.

Zaloga, Steven: *Campaign 100 D-Day 1944 (1) Omaha Beach*; Osprey, 2003.

Zaloga, Steven: *Fortress 37 D-Day Fortifications in Normandy*; Osprey, 2005.

Zaloga, Steven: *The Devil's Garden*; Stackpole Books, 2013.

Websites that provide fantastic information:
http://omahabeach.vierville.free.fr
Photosnormandie

Key to Map Symbols

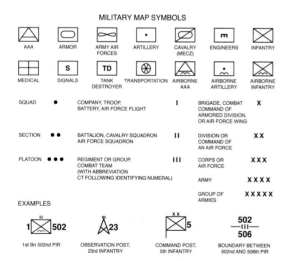